KNOTS
for Paddlers

Charlie Walbridge

Illustrations by Grant Tatum

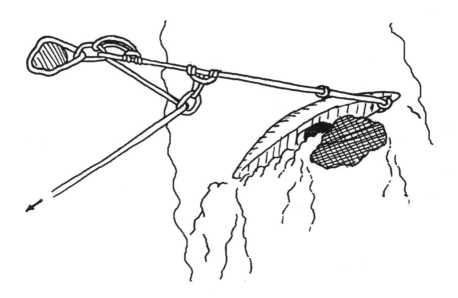

Menasha Ridge Press
Birmingham, Alabama

American Canoe Association
Springfield, Virginia

Printed in the United States of America
Published by Menasha Ridge Press
First edition, second printing

Illustrations by Grant Tatum
Text design and production
by Carolina Graphics Group

This is an instruction book for knots for canoeists and
kayakers. Paddling is inherently dangerous. You should not
depend solely on information gleaned from this book for
your personal safety. This book cannot replace an approved
and appropriate course in canoeing, swimming or lifesav-
ing.

American Canoe Association
7432 Alban Station Boulevard, Suite B-226
Springfield, Virginia 22150

Menasha Ridge Press
3169 Cahaba Heights Road
Birmingham, Alabama 35243

Contents

Introduction

The effort needed to learn a few key knots will be repaid in added confidence.

Although a book filled with pages of knots seems intimidating at first, the effort needed to learn a few key knots will be repaid in added confidence on the water. Whether you're pulling a canoe off a midstream boulder or tying a kayak to the roof of your car, the wrong knot can lead to trouble; the right knot will hold under extremely heavy loads and untie easily without damaging the rope.

This book presents eighteen of the most useful knots for paddlers and some of the practical ways they are used, such as cartopping and boat extrication. You don't have to learn all of these knots to have fun on the water, but most are valuable.

Get a short length of rope to practice the knots as you read along. After a few practice runs, try them without looking at the diagrams. Soon you'll be handling rope like a pro.

A Word About Rope

The type of rope you choose depends on how you will use it. You don't necessarily need a high strength rope to tie your boats on the car; ordinary quarter-inch nylon rope or retired rescue line will do. However, you don't want to skimp on rope quality when unpinning a boat, a process which generates thousands of pounds of stress on rope.

Material, construction, and quality affect a rope's strength, durability, and manageability. According to international standards, the minimal breaking strength for rescue line is 500 kilograms (1100 pounds). Most common rescue lines are made of three-eights-inch polypropylene with a breaking strength of 700 to 900 kilograms (1500-2000 pounds). Sometimes these ropes are reinforced with stronger fibers, such as nylon or Spectra, for added toughness and durability necessary in rescue efforts.Unlike nylon ropes, polypropylene floats and is less likely to catch on submerged snags and rocks. This makes it easier to recover.

When paddling, it's a good idea to carry a sixty- to seventy-foot length of three-eighths inch diameter polypropylene line. These compact rescue bags are often stored in protective stuff bags. There are rescue-lines on the market made especially for boaters. Though lighter, they may lack the strength to safely unpin a boat.

Ropes have the potential to be dangerous when used unwisely. Never tie yourself into a rope around moving water. If you slip into the current, you could be pulled underwater and drown. Lines can also become snagged while effecting rescue or unpin-

Ropes have the potential to be dangerous when used unwisely.

ning a boat. A rope under tension becomes as rigid and unyielding as a steel bar and can knock a person over or pin him against a tree. Never abandon rope in fast water; it can create a deadly trap for swimmers. Any line that becomes entangled during a rescue must be recovered or cut off as short as possible. Because of this danger, all paddlers should carry a readily-accessible knife. Finally, since ropes deteriorate over time, it's a good idea to replace rescue lines every few years. Recycle these as tiedowns for boats and gear.

The Knots

A Few Rope Terms:

A few terms will make knot-tying explanations easier. The **free end** is the short length at each end of the rope. The **standing part** of the rope is the center section that does the actual work. When the free end of the rope is bent back parallel to the standing part, it forms a **bight**. Cross the free end of a bight over the standing part and you've made a **loop**. When you take a loop and pass the free end through the loop and out a second time, you've made a simple **overhand knot**. All the knots in this book are made up of bights, loops, or overhand knots. Since any knot can slip under pressure (especially when tied with slippery synthetic line), leave four to six inches of the free end outside the knot to form the **tail**.

> **All the knots in this book are made up of bights, loops, or overhand knots.**

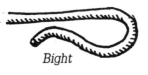
Bight

Overhand Knot

Loop

Knots for Car-Topping

Two Half Hitches

This popular knot is used to tie off the end of a line
when mooring a boat or tying it to the roof of your
car.

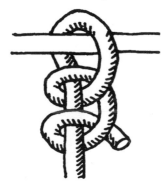

- Form a bight by passing the rope through or around the point of
  attachment.

- Loop the free end around the standing part of the rope, passing the end
  to the inside. Slide the hitch down so that it is tight against the object
  you're tying onto. This is a **Single Half Hitch**.

- Repeat the process, placing the second loop on the outside of the first.
  Push this loop tight against the first loop.

- To untie, undo the outer loop, then pull back on the free end to loosen the
  inner loop.

Bowline

A bowline creates a loop of any size at the end of a line that will not slip closed under tension. It's designed to create a waist loop in a rescue line, but it's also useful when tying a rope to a roof rack upright.

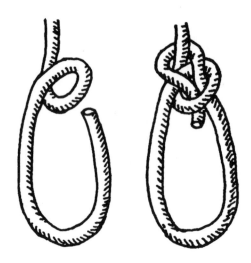

- Create a loop in the standing part of the line, with the free end crossing over the top.

- Push the free end of the rope up through the loop, wrap it around the standing part, then pull it back through the loop. Set the knot tight.

- Many people remember this knot by saying: "The rabbit goes in the hole, around the tree, and back in the hole again." The "hole" is the loop and the "tree" is the standing part of the rope. Remember that the "tree" has "roots" that must go under the free end.

- To untie a bowline, push the loop of rope over the standing end. Twist the tail to make the rope diameter smaller, then push it out the "rabbit hole."

Trucker's Hitch

The trucker's hitch is a good choice for anyone who needs to secure a load. It is especially suited to tying large numbers of boats securely to a cartop rack.

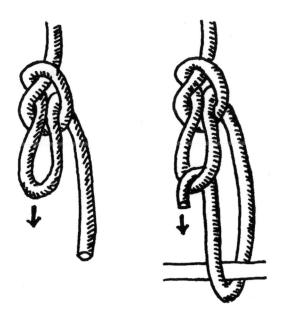

- Create a loop on the standing end, with the free end on top.

- Push a bight of rope from the free end through the loop and pull down, cinching the loop tightly around it. (Do *not* make the bight from the standing end; it will tighten up and bind the rope when pressure is applied.)

- Pass the free end around an anchor point, then run it back through the loop formed by the bight.

- Pull down on the free end. This creates a two-to-one mechanical advantage and allows you to pull the rope very tight.

- Tie off with two half hitches.

Taut-Line Hitch

A taut-line hitch is easily tightened or loosened without being retied. It was designed to keep a tent rope under tension and is perfect for use on the front and back end lines when cartopping boats.

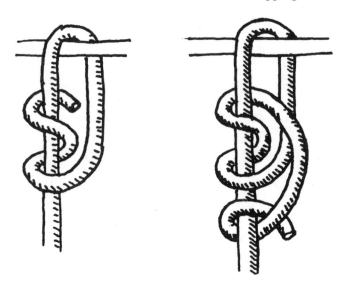

- Create a bight by passing the free end of the rope around an anchor point and bring it back up parallel to the standing part.

- Wrap the free end two or three times around the standing part of the rope, then pull it away from the anchor. This creates a loop around the anchor point.

- Tie a single half hitch around the standing part of the rope with the free end just outside the anchor loop.

- To adjust the loop, hold the knot in one hand and pull the rope through from one end or the other.

Sheet Bend and Double Sheet Bend

The sheet bend and its cousin, the double sheet bend, are used to connect two ropes of the same or different thicknesses. This comes in handy when getting the extra length needed to tie large numbers of boats to your car.

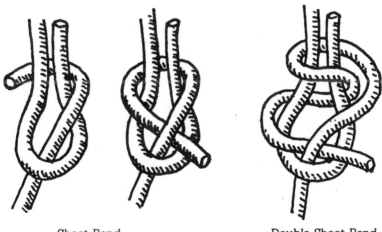

Sheet Bend   Double Sheet Bend

- Make a bight in the thicker of the two ropes to be joined.

- To finish the sheet bend, pass the free end of the second rope through the center of the bight, under and around it, then tuck it under the standing part of the second rope. Pull the knot tight, leaving a four- to six-inch tail.

- For extra security, tie a double sheet bend. Pass the free end of the second rope through the center of the bight, then over and around it. Now, run the line under the standing part and around the bight, then back under the standing part a second time. Pull the knot snug, leaving a four- to six-inch tail.

Knots for River Rescue

The Figure 8 Family of Knots

A figure 8 reduces a line's strength less than any other knot.

If you only want to learn one knot, consider the figure 8. With variations on this versatile knot, you can make a hand or waist loop, join two ropes, or create attachment points on a hauling line or Z-Drag. While any knot weakens a rope, a figure 8 reduces a line's strength less than any other. It is easily untied, even after being pulled very tight.

Straight Figure 8

This is the basic knot, used as a "stopper" in rescue bags. It's really an overhand knot with an extra twist that reduces stress on the rope and makes it easier to untie.

■ Create a loop in the line, then take the free end around the standing part of the rope and up through the loop. Pull until snug.

Figure 8 on a Bight

This knot is used to create a loop that will not get smaller as tension is applied to the line.

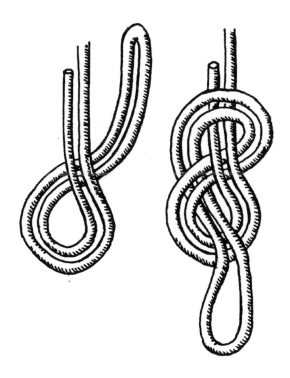

- Double the rope over to form a bight, then create a loop with the doubled rope.

- Take the free end of the doubled rope around the standing part, and up through the loop. Pull until snug.

Figure 8 Follow-Through

There are two versions of this knot; each has a different function. One allows you to join two lines; the other permits you to create a loop of any size in the end of the rope. It's a bit slower to tie than a bowline, but just as effective.

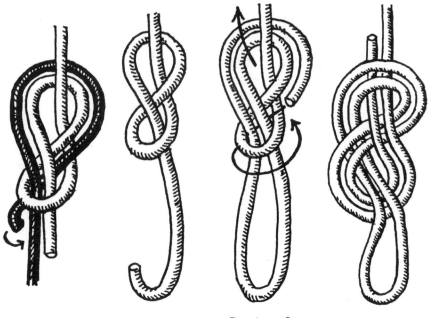

Joining Two Lines   *Creating a Loop*

- To join two lines together, create a figure 8 at the end of one line.

- Starting at the free end of the first rope, retrace its path with the free end of the second line. Leave a tail of four to six inches at each end.

- To create a loop around your waist, tie a figure 8 three to four feet from one end of the line.

- Pass the other end around your waist, then retrace the figure 8 that end. Leave a tail of four to six inches.

Directional Figure 8

This useful knot creates loops that can be used to create handholds on a hauling line. It also provides a place to attach a Z-Drag to the line when prussiks are unavailable.

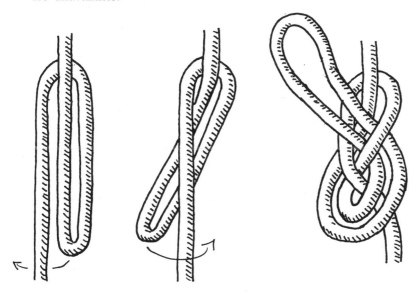

- Holding a line attached to an object (the standing part), take a bight of rope and create a loop by passing rope beneath the standing part of the line. Next pass the end of the bight around the rope, then back through the loop.

- To untie any figure 8, break the knot by pushing the outer coil of rope over the end loop, turn the knot over, and push the loops over the standing part. Repeat as needed. This loosens the knot so that it can be pulled apart.

Knots for Making Anchors

Anchors create secure attachment points for the Z-Drag and other systems used to rescue boats. All of them require a continuous loop of rope or webbing. Here's how to make these loops:

Water Knot

The water knot ties two ends of a length of webbing together, forming a continuous loop. Many paddlers make a loop of rope or webbing just long enough to wear around their waist like a belt, cinching the ends with a carabiner. This loop makes a useful leash for dragging your boat along on portages, and can be used to create anchor points for boat recovery systems. If worn on the waist, keep it snug to minimize entanglement risk.

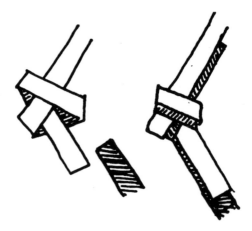

- Tie an overhand knot on one end of the webbing.

- Have the other end retrace the overhand knot in the opposite direction. The tails should exit from opposite sides of the knot, and should be four to six inches long.

- Adjust the size of the webbing loop, then pull the knot tight to set it.

Girth Hitch

A girth hitch is used to cinch a continuous loop around a log, rock, or other anchor when it is important that the anchor loop hold securely. Because stress is concentrated at the sharp bends of the hitch, it is not as strong as simply wrapping a line with a loop at the end around an anchor and connecting the ends with a carabiner.

Weak Point

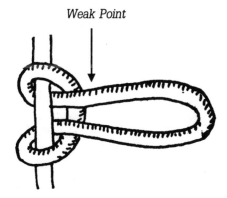

■ Lay the loop across the rock or anchor you want to attach it to. Pass one end of the loop through the other end and pull back on it until the hitch is snug.

Fisherman's Knot

The double fisherman's knot is the most secure way to tie two lengths of rope together. It gets its name because fishermen use it to join two lengths of slippery monofilament line. Paddlers use it to create grab loops on whitewater boats, Prusik loops for hauling systems, and large continuous loops for anchors.

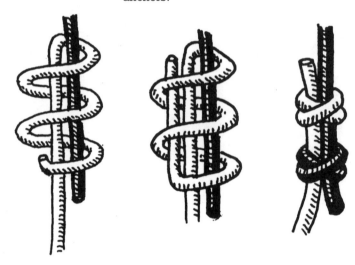

- Lay two ropes side-by-side, their ends pointing in opposite directions. You'll need about eighteen inches of free end on each rope.

- Moving toward the second line's free end, wrap the free end of the first line twice around the standing part of the second so that the coils wrap around both ropes. Push the free end through the center of the coils, leaving a four- to six-inch tail.

- Repeat by wrapping the second line around the first in the opposite direction and on the other side, then push the free end through the coils. Tighten the knot by pulling the standing ends of both ropes. The knots should slide snugly against each other before tightening down.

For a double or triple fisherman's knot use one or two more wraps of rope, respectively. A double is used with nylon or polypropylene. A triple is reccomended with slippery Spectra line.

Knots for Controlling a Rope

When the pull on a line becomes too strong to hold, there are various knots and hitches that can help maintain your grip.

Muenter Hitch

The muenter hitch creates considerable friction, allowing the user to let out line under tension in a controlled way. Paddlers often use it to lower boats down steep slopes at remote put-ins. It is most effective when used with an oversized pear-shaped carabiner, but, if done correctly, it will work with any oval-shaped locking carabiner

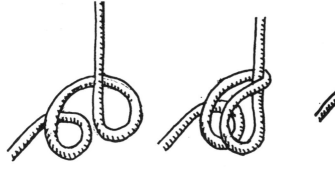

- Make two loops of rope. The inside line should be on top of one loop and on the bottom of the other.

- Fold the two loops into each other and clip a locking carabiner into both loops.

- Pull line through the muenter hitch in either direction; the load is on the section of line under the friction loop.

- When reversing directions, the hitch will flip over so that the friction loop passes over the other side of the rig.

Prusik Knot

The prusik knot is used to attach a continuous loop of line to a second rope. The line used for the prusik loop should be roughly half the thickness of the line it's being used with; a three-eighths inch (roughly 10mm) throw line requires a prusik loop made from 5mm line. A prusik knot will bite into the larger rope and hold when under tension, yet slide easily when the load is released. It is used to help create a Z-Drag, the most common hauling system used to recover pinned boats in whitewater.

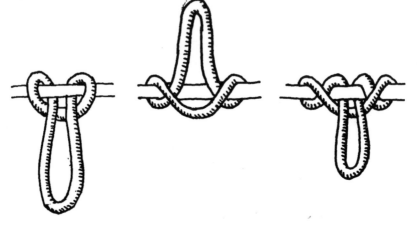

- Start with a prusik loop, a loop of line roughly twenty-four inches long. Make this from an appropriately-sized five-foot length of line, joining the ends with a double fisherman's knot.

- Lay the loop across the line you plan to attach to, with the fisherman's knot halfway down one side of the loop.

- Pass one loop end through the other loop end. Wrap the loop around the line and pass through the other loop once more.

- Pull the loop snug, tightening the knot. "Dress" the knot so that the coils lie neatly side-by-side. Pull down at right angles to the knot, tightening it further until it grips the rope securely. This helps the prusik achieve the maximum possible hold.

Knots for Mooring a Boat

These knots hold a line securely, yet will release with a single tug on the free end. They are also helpful in rescues, either when towing swamped boats to shore or anchoring safety lines attached to pinned boats.

Hitching Tie

This is a fancy name for a simple slip knot used in pre-automotive days to tie up horses.

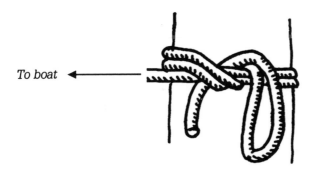

To boat ←

- Take a bight of rope and pass it around a tree or other object, next tie an overhand knot on the standing part of the line; leaving the free end sticking out. *Note:* The direction of pull must come from the same side as the free end.

- To release, pull on the free end.

Clove Hitch and Slippery Clove Hitch

The clove hitch is a more secure way of mooring a boat to a tree or dock. The slippery clove hitch is a quick-release knot that holds no matter what the direction of pull.

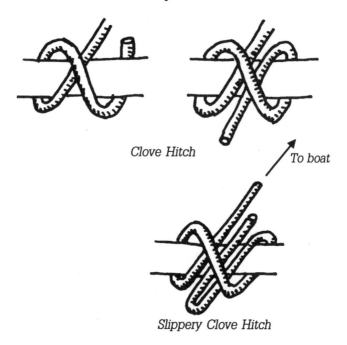

Clove Hitch

To boat

Slippery Clove Hitch

- Wrap the line once around an upright, crossing the free end over the standing part of the rope.

- Wrap the line a second time, this time passing the free end *under* the standing part.

- To make the clove hitch a quick-release knot, tie as before, but on the second wrap pass a bight of rope under the standing part of the rope. The free end should form a tail of eighteen inches or more once the knot is cinched.

- To release, pull on the free end. The rope will pull free easily.

Using Knots

Cartopping Boats

Using your car to carry canoes and kayaks to the water is part of almost any paddling trip. Cartopping is easy, but carelessness may have serious consequences; losing a boat off the roof of a car is no laughing matter. Even if no other vehicles are hit, your boat will probably be damaged or destroyed.

Before you buy a rack, know the capacity of your vehicle. Many modern cars are not designed to carry loads on the roof, and not all factory roof-racks can't be trusted to carry boats. Finding the right rack takes time, and a good strong one is not inexpensive. It pays to consult the rack fit tables at your local outfitting shop before purchasing your next vehicle.

Once you have your racks, consider the spacing or spread of the rack's crossbar: the wider apart the crossbars, the more stable the load. A spread of four or five feet is ideal; a three-foot spread is recommended for boats over fourteen feet long, while a two-foot width works well enough for shorter boats. Also keep the weight capacity of the rack in mind, especially with multiple-boat loads.

No matter what type of rack you use, end lines are always a good idea. As you drive down the road, the air tends to lift the boat, putting enormous pressures on the tie downs. Tie the boats to the racks, then tie bow and stern lines to the bumper as backup.

Finding a place to tie the end lines is sometimes difficult. Older cars have many possibilities, but modern aerodynamic bumpers offer few potential attachment points. Look behind the bumper and try to attach the line to the frame. Many vehicles have

Cartopping is easy, but carelessness may have serious consequences.

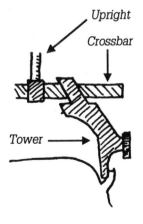

Upright

Crossbar

Tower

"towing attachments" under the front and rear bumpers. Make sure what you tie into is strong enough to hold the load and has no sharp edges that could cut the rope. Don't tie into the shock absorbers, springs, or steering arms.

There are many variations to cartopping. What follows are a few ways to tie down single or multiple boats safely and securely.

One final warning: As the load bounces and shifts, it exploits any weaknesses in your tiedowns. The boat may work loose despite your best efforts. Keep a close eye on the load! If you hear knocking or bouncing, or if the boat seems loose or assumes unexpected positions, stop and inspect your cargo. Correct any problems before continuing on.

To load a single boat on your car:

- Place the canoe or kayak to one side, next to one of the uprights. This will prevent the boat from being pushed from side to side when the vehicle is moving.

- Tie a **bowline** around the tower to one side of the boat. Pass the line over the boat, around the rack's crossbar, and back to the tower.

- Pull the line snug and tie with **two half hitches**. For a very secure tie use a **trucker's hitch**. But beware: a trucker's hitch can generate enough pressure to crush a kayak or lightweight canoe! Watch the hull carefully and stop pulling if it starts to flex and crack.

- Repeat the process for the other crossbar.

- Attach a line to the front of the boat and secure it to the front bumper of the car with a **taut-line hitch**. Do the same thing in back.

Two kayaks can be loaded side-by-side; anchor each boat to a tower as described above. For three or more kayaks, load them on their side. This takes up less space. An upright bar purchased with your rack will facilitate this loading. Two canoes can also be tied on this way if the bar is wide enough. If the bar is too narrow to load the canoes side by side, secure the first canoe to the crossbars as described above. Next, lean the second canoe up on the first so that one gunwale rests on the bar, and the other rests on the first canoe. Tie to racks as you would a single boat.

Kayaks can also be leaned up against an open canoe or kayak that has already been tied in place, as follows:

- Tie a **bowline** to a tower outside the last kayak.

- Pass the rope over the kayaks, around the crossbar and back to the tower. Secure with **two half hitches**.

- Pass the rope over the entire load, and secure with a **trucker's hitch**. You can pull much harder on side-loaded kayaks than flat-loaded ones.

- Repeat the process for the other crossbar.

- For end lines, put a loop on the end of a line with a **figure 8 on a bight**. Run the rope through both grab loops, then through the loop to create a noose. Tighten the noose to pull the two ends of the boat toward each other, then tie it off with a **single half hitch**. Secure the other end to the vehicle with a **taut-line hitch.** Repeat for the other end.

You've probably seen pictures of cars carrying two canoes with more boats on top, or a van piled with eight or more kayaks. To manage this load, set up the first "layer" of boats as described above. When the bottom layer is secure, more boats can be piled on top. The lightest and most fragile boats should always be carried on top. Next, throw tiedowns over the entire load and pull each one tight with a **trucker's hitch**. Then run a length of rope between the front end loops of all the boats. Loop the ends together, tighten, the secure the line to the front end of the car. Repeat this process at the back of the vehicle. Drive with caution when loaded this way, especially on turns and in crosswinds.

Occasionally you may have to carry a boat without a roof rack.

Occasionally you may have to carry a boat without a roof rack. Here's how to secure the boat to the roof of a car or other vehicle:

- First, pad the roof to protect it from abrasion. Some people use blankets or sleeping pads, but these offer minimal protection. Foam pads are available commercially and work well.

- Place your boat on the roof and check for fit. Kayaks can be carried either upside down or right-side up. Open canoes are always carried upside down. If the roof buckles, carrying the boat this way may damage the car.

- Run a safety line around the boat and in through the car doors, using a **trucker's hitch** to cinch it tight. Slam the doors shut. On two-door vehicles this line will probably get in the driver's way. If it does, you'll have to do without a safety line.

- Bow and stern lines do most of the job of holding the boat on the roof. The lines should run from the bow and stern grab loops to the corners of their respective bumpers. Loop the line once around the grab loop so the boat won't slip from side to side. Secure both sides of the front and rear lines with **trucker's hitches**. Watch the roof carefully, and back off on the tension if it begins to bend. Tuck in the edges of blankets or foam sheets to keep them from flapping.

Boat Extrication

Thanks to the almost universal use of flotation bags, modern canoes, kayaks and self-bailing rafts are not easily pinned. But when they do wrap, it's going to be a humdinger! Unpinning a boat demands that paddlers work with the river. This requires a knowledge of how the water works and an appreciation of how to apply force effectively.

Unpinning a boat demands that paddlers work with the river.

The Pinning Mechanism

The first step is to determine the mechanism of the pin. The rescuer's job is to figure out which end of the boat is under the least pressure from the water and then move that end. This allows water to push the other end downstream, pivoting the craft off the rock to freedom. There are three basic types of pins.

A CENTER PIN occurs when a canoe or kayak impacts a rock amidships and wraps around it. The boat stays pinned because the pressure is roughly equal on each side of the boat. Your job is to upset the balance. In an END-TO-END PIN, the bow and the stern of a craft are hung up on separate rocks. One end must be lifted free to recover the boat. VERTICAL PINS may occur when a paddler is running a steep ledge. The bow dives deep and hangs up behind an underwater rock at the base of the drop. The stern settles back against the ledge, and the boat is stuck. In vertical pins, the boat can be pulled backwards, away from the "piton" rock, or pulled out forward, end-over-end.

Setting Anchors

Often a pinned canoe or kayak can be freed with muscle power, but when that fails, mechanical advantage systems can be used.

To apply mechanical advantage, you need a solid anchor.

To apply mechanical advantage, you need a solid anchor. This can be constructed from a webbing loop wrapped around a rock or tree and clipped into itself. Make sure that the loop is long enough so that the inside angle at the point of the pull is under ninety degrees. A greater angle increases stress on the webbing and can cause it to break.

If you're tying into trees and shrubs, place the anchor as low as possible. If the anchor sits higher it creates considerable leverage on the roots. When the anchor is near the ground, surprisingly scruffy bushes may be sufficient.

You can also place a loop directly over a rock projection or stump. A loop can be **girth hitched** around a rock or log which is wedged behind a crack or opening between rocks. It can also be cinched around a point where two rocks are jammed together. This is known as a **chock**. If a crack is very narrow, the webbing or line can be passed through it and the knot itself will serve as a chock.

Safety Precautions

The forces created in extricating a boat are enormous. Pulling on a rope stores considerable force in the line. Z-drags have been known to dislodge seemingly steady trees and boulders. Should the rope break, it will snap back like a giant rubber band, pulling hardware with it. The force of this "kickback" can take the bark off trees! Here are some ways you can protect yourself.

■ Always wear your life vest and helmet.

■ Test the anchor by pulling hard on the loop. Remember, even seemingly steady trees and boulders can be dislodged, so choose your anchor carefully.

- Don't look down the rope as you pull. A boater stationed off to one side can tell you how the rescue is coming.

- If the anchor point is a tall rock or tree, pulling from directly behind it offers some protection.

- If the anchor offers no protection, you can redirect the pull. Using a length of webbing as anchor, place it with a carabiner directly in line with the haul rope. The rope then passes through the carabiner and off to the side where your group can operate in safety.

- Hanging a weight from the line a third of the way to the pinned boat can catch and redirect much of the force of the kickback. Attach a prusik loop to the haul line, then hang a rescue bag or a couple of canteens from it.

- Tying a life vest around the haul line offers some kickback protection, but we don't recommend it. The last thing you want is somebody running around a rescue site without a life vest!

Attaching a Hauling Line

Since rope systems are time-consuming to set up, paddlers should first try to lift the boat free directly. Always tie a safety line to one end of the boat and securely anchor it on shore. Without this anchor, a pinned boat full of water may be uncontrollable in fast current. What is the good of pulling a boat free, only to have it carried downstream into a worse situation?

If this doesn't work, tie a line to the boat and have a group of people on shore attempt to pull it free. The angle of the pull is very important. A rope is most effective when pulling at a right angle to the keel line of the pinned boat. Unfortunately, the shoreline seldom cooperates. A good setup is to attach a rope to the end of the boat farthest away from your position, crossing the river at a forty-five degree angle to the length of the boat. A **no knot**, set behind a group of people hauling on the line, can be adjusted after each pull to take up the slack and keep the line tight during rest breaks.

No Knot

Don't be stubborn. If pulling on one end of the boat doesn't work, try working on the other end from the opposite shore. As a last resort, mechanical advantage systems can be employed.

There are numerous variations of these hauling systems, but space does not permit detailing them here. Just remember to keep your rig simple. Friction builds as a hauling system becomes more complex, and efficiency is lost with each bend in the rope. Unless you use plenty of rescue pulleys and are very careful when rigging the system, it will eventually bind up.

The Z-Drag

A Z-Drag is a three-to-one mechanical advantage hauling system that can be set up with a few lightweight tools easily carried by paddlers. You'll need a webbing loop to serve as an anchor, two Prusik loops, and three carabiners. Pulleys can be attached to the carabiners to reduce friction in the system, but they don't increase the efficiency much. Here's what to do:

- (1) Set the anchor using a webbing loop and a carabiner. This carabiner becomes the anchor carabiner. The haul line should be set across the current at a forty-five degree angle to the length of the hull.

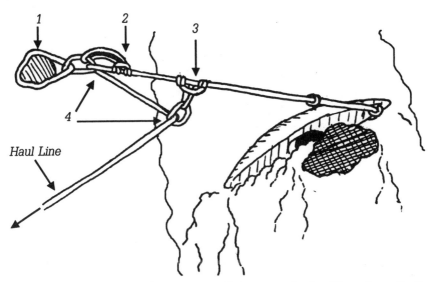

■ (2) Using a **prusik loop**, tie a **prusik knot** on the haul line, then clip the loop into the anchor carabiner. This is the **brake prusik**. If you have a second webbing loop available, the **haul line** and the **brake prusik** can be anchored separately.

■ (3) Using a **prusik loop**, tie a second **prusik knot** ahead of the first. This is the **traveling prusik**.

■ (4) The haul line goes through the anchor carabiner, then through a second carabiner attached to the **traveling prusik**. This creates the characteristic "Z" shape of the hauling rig.

■ Take out the slack in the haul line, moving the **brake prusik** forward to keep it tight. Now push the **traveling prusik** as far forward as possible. The system is ready for the pull to begin.

■ As the haul line is pulled in, advance the **brake prusik**. This creates a ratchet effect, holding the line firmly between pulls and allowing the group to take rest breaks.

■ When the **traveling prusik** gets pulled so close to the **brake prusik** that further pulling is impossible, transfer the tension in the line to the **brake prusik**. Then push the **traveling prusik** as far out on the line as possible and resume the pull.

A prusik will begin to slip at about eight hundred pounds of pressure. This is a sure sign that you are approaching the working limits of most rescue ropes and caution is advised. If you are close to success, see if dressing the traveling prusik further will provide enough extra bite to succeed.

Making a Haul Rig Without Tools

A similar system can be set up without Prusiks. It works very well using the one-fourth inch Spectra line often carried by kayakers. This is less effective and much harder on the rope, and should be used only when heavier rope is unavailable.

- Place one or two **directional figure 8's** as far out on the rope as possible, pointing towards the direction of pull.

- Set an anchor as with the Z-Drag (above) using a webbing loop and a carabiner.

- Clip a carabiner into one of the **directional figure 8's**. Don't try to pull the rope through the loop by itself; the heat of friction will probably burn it through.

- Run the haul line through the anchor carabiner, then through the carabiner attached to the **directional figure 8**. You now have a Z-Drag. Tension the system and start pulling.

The disadvantage of this system is that you can only pull in a limited amount of rope. Once the directional figure 8 reaches the anchor you can pull no more, and the system must be dismantled and set up again. Another drawback is the lack of a braking system to hold the line tight between pulls.